TOSEL®
READING SERIES

BASIC

READING

1

ITC International TOSEL Committee

KB006951

CONTENTS

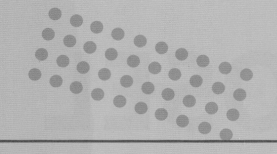

About TOSEL®

TOSEL (Test of Skills in the English Language) was developed to meet the demand for a more effective assessment of English as a foreign language for learners from specific cultural settings.

TOSEL evaluates and certifies the proficiency levels of English learners, from the age of 4 through adulthood, along with academic and job performance results.

Background

- Other English tests are ineffective in accurately measuring individual abilities
- Overuse of US-dominated testing systems in diverse cultural and educational contexts in the global English language learning market

Functions & Usage

- Assessment is categorized into 7 levels
- Used as a qualification for academic excellence for school admissions
- Used as a test to assess the English proficiency in the corporate and public sectors

Goals

- Create an effective tool for assessing and evaluating the English skills of English language learners
- Implement efficient and accessible testing systems and methods
- Provide constructive and developmental English education guidance

TOSEL® Strength

LEVELED ASSESSMENTS

An established English test system fit for seven different levels according to learners' cognitive development

ACCURATE DIAGNOSIS

A systematic and scientific diagnosis of learners' English proficiency

EXTENSIVE MATERIALS

Supplementary materials to help learners in an EFL environment to prepare for TOSEL and improve their proficiency

SUFFICIENT DATA

Content for each level developed by using data accumulated from more than 2,000,000 TOSEL test takers delegated at 15,000 schools and academies

CLASSIFIED AREAS OF INTELLIGENCE

Content designed to foster and expand the strengths of each student, categorized by the eight areas of intelligence

CONTINUITY

A complete course of English education ranging from kindergarten, elementary school, middle school, high schoool, and up to adults.

HIGH RELIABILITY

A high reliability level (Cronbach's alpha: .904 for elementary school students / .864 for university students) proven by several studies (Oxford University / Modern Language Journal)

SYSTEMATIC & EFFECTIVE ENGLISH EDUCATION

Accurate diagnosis and extensive materials which provide a step-by-step development in English learning, according to the quality of each learner's ability

TOSEL® Level Chart

Seven Separate Assessments

TOSEL divides the test into seven stages, by considering the test takers' cognitive levels, according to different ages. Unlike other assessments based on only one level, TOSEL includes separate assessments for preschool, elementary school, middle school, high school students, and for adults, which also includes both professionals and college students.

TOSEL's reporting system highlights the strengths and weaknesses of each test taker and suggests areas for further development.

COCOON

Suitable for children aged 4-6 (pre-schoolers)

The first step in the TOSEL system, the test is composed of colorful designs and interesting questions to interest young learners and to put them at ease.

Pre-STARTER

Suitable for children aged 7-8 (1st-2nd grades of elementary school)

Evaluates the ability to comprehend simple vocabulary, conversations, and sentences.

STARTER

Suitable for children aged 9-10 (3rd-4th grades of elementary school)

Evaluates the ability to comprehend short sentences and conversations related to everyday situations or topics.

BASIC

Suitable for children aged 11-12 (5th-6th grades of elementary school)

Evaluates the ability to communicate about personal information, daily activities, future plans, and past experiences in written and spoken language.

JUNIOR

Suitable for middle school students

Evaluates the ability to comprehend short paragraphs, practical texts, and speech covering general topics and to participate in simple daily conversations.

HIGH JUNIOR

Suitable for high school students

Evaluates the ability to use English fluently, accurately, and effectively on a wide range of social and academic subjects, as well as the ability to use sentences with a variety of complex structures.

ADVANCED

Suitable for university students and adults

Evaluates the ability to use practical English required for a job or work environment, as well as the ability to use and understand English at the university level.

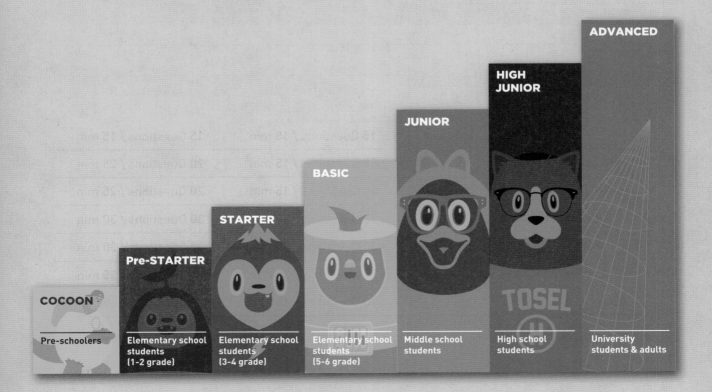

Evaluation

Assessing the Four Skills

TOSEL evaluates the four language skills: reading, listening, speaking and writing, through indirect and direct assessment items.

This system of evaluation is part of a concerted effort to break away from materials geared solely toward grammar and reading-oriented education.

TOSEL Test Information

Level	Score	Grade	Section	
			Section I Listening & Speaking	Section II Reading & Writing
COCOON	100		15 Questions / 15 min	15 Questions / 15 min
Pre-STARTER	100		15 Questions / 15 min	20 Questions / 25 min
STARTER	100		20 Questions / 15 min	20 Questions / 25 min
BASIC	100	1-10	30 Questions / 20 min	30 Questions / 30 min
JUNIOR	100		30 Questions / 20 min	30 Questions / 30 min
HIGH JUNIOR	100		30 Questions / 25 min	35 Questions / 35 min
ADVANCED	990		70 Questions / 45 min	70 Questions / 55 min

Certificates

TOSEL Certificate

The International TOSEL Committee officially evaluates and certifies the level of English proficiency of English learners from the age of 4 to adults.

Certified by

Mar. 2010   Korea University
Dec. 2009   The Korean Society of Speech Science
Dec. 2009   The Korea Association of Foreign Language Education
Nov. 2009   The Applied Linguistics Association of Korea
Oct. 2009   The Pan Korea English Teachers Association

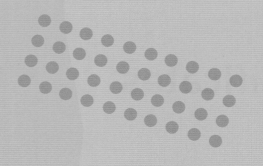

CHAPTER 1

Neighbors

UNIT 1

My Perfect Neighborhood

Teacher's Book
p.44

Who lives in your neighborhood?

UNIT 1 My Perfect Neighborhood

I love my neighborhood. It is safe and quiet. My neighbors care about each other. They always try to help. One day my father's car broke down. Ms. Pitafi came and fixed it. I think she is very kind. Another time, Ms. Filio's cat ran away. My father walked around the neighborhood to help her. He walked around for more than an hour. Finally, he found the cat. There are also many police officers in my neighborhood. They help people with problems. Sometimes they help wild animals. They mostly walk or drive around the neighborhood to help us. So I don't worry about going outside late at night. Lastly, there aren't many cars on the road. People usually take the bus to go to school or work. This is why my neighborhood is quiet. We don't have to worry about cars! The quiet neighborhood lets me sleep well at night. My neighborhood is perfect. I want to live here forever.

New Words

your neighborhood

n the streets near your home

neighbor

n a person living near your home

care about

v think about people's feelings

break down

v stop working

kind

adj nice

worry about

v think about with some fear

Part A. Sentence Completion

1. I played chess _____ two hours.

    (A) at

    (B) on

    (C) for

    (D) while

2. There are many police _____ in our town.

    (A) car

    (B) a car

    (C) officer

    (D) officers

Part B. Situational Writing

3.

    They walk _____.

    (A) at noon

    (B) late at night

    (C) in the afternoon

    (D) late in the morning

4.

    Jinhee is _____ a red car.

    (A) fixing

    (B) selling

    (C) buying

    (D) driving

Buildings	Location	Phone Number
Lux Theater	Q Street	234-5678
Chaut Art Gallery	Holdridge Avenue	111-2323
Salton Library	Saint Paul Avenue	055-2434
Parkins Clothes Store	North 34th Street	277-8603
Huskers Bank	Vine Street	922-5678

5. Which building is on Vine Street?

(A) Lux Theater

(B) Huskers Bank

(C) Salton Library

(D) Chaut Art Gallery

6. What number should you probably call if you want to buy a dress?

(A) 234-5678

(B) 055-2434

(C) 277-8603

(D) 922-5678

Part D. General Reading and Retelling

I love my neighborhood. It is safe and quiet. My neighbors care about each other. They always try to help. One day my father's car broke down. Ms. Pitafi came and fixed it. I think she is very kind. Another time, Ms. Filio's cat ran away. My father walked around the neighborhood to help her. He walked around for more than an hour. Finally, he found the cat. There are also many police officers in my neighborhood. They help people with problems. Sometimes they help wild animals. They mostly walk or drive around the neighborhood to help us. So I don't worry about going outside late at night. Lastly, there aren't many cars on the road. People usually take the bus to go to school or work. This is why my neighborhood is quiet. We don't have to worry about cars! The quiet neighborhood lets me sleep well at night. My neighborhood is perfect. I want to live here forever.

7. What is the main idea of the passage?

(A) My neighborhood is great.

(B) I hate noisy neighborhoods.

(C) People should buy more cars.

(D) Neighbors should help each other.

8. Who is Ms. Pitafi, probably?

(A) the writer

(B) the writer's sister

(C) the writer's mother

(D) the writer's neighbor

9. What do police officers NOT do in this neighborhood?

(A) help wild animals

(B) drive buses to work

(C) help people who are in trouble

(D) walk around the neighborhood

10. What happened to Ms. Filio?

(A) She lost her dog.

(B) Her cat ran away.

(C) Her car broke down.

(D) She caught a wild animal.

Listening Practice

 Listen and write.

  MP3 B1-1

My Perfect Neighborhood

I love my neighborhood. It is safe and quiet. My ¹ _____ ² _____ about each other. They always try to help. One day my father's car ³ _____ . Ms. Pitafi came and fixed it. I think she is very ⁴ _____ . Another time, Ms. Filio's cat ran away. My father walked around the neighborhood to help her. He walked around for more than an hour. Finally, he found the cat. There are also many police officers in my neighborhood. They help people with problems. Sometimes they help wild animals. They mostly walk or drive around the neighborhood to help us. So I don't ⁵ _____ about going outside late at night. Lastly, there aren't many cars on the road. People usually take the bus to go to school or work. This is why my ⁶ _____ is quiet. We don't have to worry about cars! The quiet neighborhood lets me sleep well at night. My neighborhood is perfect. I want to live here forever.

Word Bank

kind	nayborhood	neighborhood
worry	kindd	naybors
warry	care	cere
neighbors	broke down	brake down

 Listen. Pause. Say each sentence.

  MP3 B1-1G

Writing Practice

 Write the words.

your ¹ _____
[n] the streets near your home

2 _____
[n] a person living near your home

3 _____
[v] think about people's feelings

4 _____
[v] stop working

5 _____
[adj] nice

6 _____
[v] think about with some fear

 Write the words in each blank.

Summary

I love my neighborhood. My _____ help people and animals. There
are also police _____ in the neighborhood. Also, my neighborhood
_____ quiet. I want to _____ here forever!

Word Puzzle

 Complete the word puzzle.

1↓ nice

2→ stop working

3↓ the streets near your home

4→ think about people's feelings

5→ think about with some fear

6→ a person living near your home

UNIT 2

Teacher's Book
p.48

Asking People about Jobs

Think! You are thirty years old.
Do you have a job? What do you do?

My teacher gave us some fun homework last week. We had to talk to different people about their jobs. First, I made a list of people. Then, I decided to talk to Mr. Moreno, Ms. Adame, Ms. Mayo, and Mr. Kinny. Mr. Moreno is a photographer. He takes pet pictures. He sees many dogs and cats every day. I went to his studio. He showed me cool cameras. Ms. Adame works at a restaurant. She brings food to customers. She loves to talk to them. She said it is fun to hear different stories. Ms. Mayo is a teacher. She teaches first and third grade math. Her students are very smart. They read a lot. Lastly, Mr. Kinny is a police officer. He protects the town every day. He wears a cool uniform to work. I spoke to these four people. Then I wrote a short essay about my future job. I want to meet many people, like Ms. Adame does. I also want to help others, like Mr. Kinny does. Oh, I don't know what I want to do!

New Words

photographer *n* His job is taking pictures. He is a <u>photographer</u>. 	**customer** *n* **ex** A <u>customer</u> buys things in stores.
police officer *n* They keep the town safe. They are <u>police officers</u>. 	**protect** *v* keep people safe
uniform *n* clothes for work, school, or sports These are <u>uniforms</u>. 	**decide** *v* choose

Part A. Sentence Completion

1. Ian gave _____ a box of chocolates.

    (A) me
    (B) we
    (C) my
    (D) our

2. My mom works _____ a restaurant. She is a cook.

    (A) at
    (B) to
    (C) on
    (D) around

Part B. Situational Writing

3.

    Ms. Davis teaches _____ students.

    (A) five
    (B) six
    (C) ten
    (D) twelve

4.

    Nick is _____ a picture of the dinner menu.

    (A) doing
    (B) taking
    (C) making
    (D) painting

Students' Future Dream Jobs

Police Officer

Teacher

Pianist

Cook

President

Writer

5. How many students want to become writers?

(A) 2

(B) 3

(C) 4

(D) 5

6. What do most of the students want to be?

(A) cooks

(B) writers

(C) teachers

(D) presidents

Part D. General Reading and Retelling

My teacher gave us some fun homework last week. We had to talk to different people about their jobs. First, I made a list of people. Then, I decided to talk to Mr. Moreno, Ms. Adame, Ms. Mayo, and Mr. Kinny. Mr. Moreno is a photographer. He takes pet pictures. He sees many dogs and cats every day. I went to his studio. He showed me cool cameras. Ms. Adame works at a restaurant. She brings food to customers. She loves to talk to them. She said it is fun to hear different stories. Ms. Mayo is a teacher. She teaches first and third grade math. Her students are very smart. They read a lot. Lastly, Mr. Kinny is a police officer. He protects the town every day. He wears a cool uniform to work. I spoke to these four people. Then I wrote a short essay about my future job. I want to meet many people, like Ms. Adame does. I also want to help others, like Mr. Kinny does. Oh, I don't know what I want to do!

7. What is the best title for the passage?

   (A) Ms. Mayo Is Very Smart
   (B) I Want to Protect My Town
   (C) Where to Buy New Cameras
   (D) Talking to Four People about Jobs

8. Why did the writer ask people questions?

   (A) to find a job
   (B) to join a club
   (C) to do some homework
   (D) to meet friends' parents

9. Which person probably sees many dogs?

   (A) Mr. Moreno
   (B) Ms. Adame
   (C) Ms. Mayo
   (D) Mr. Kinny

10. Which of the following did the writer do last?

    (A) visit a studio
    (B) write an essay
    (C) make a list of people
    (D) ask people questions

Listening Practice

 Listen and write.

  MP3 B1-2

Asking People about Jobs

My teacher gave us some fun homework last week. We had to talk to different people about their jobs. First, I made a list of people. Then, I ¹ _____ to talk to Mr. Moreno, Ms. Adame, Ms. Mayo, and Mr. Kinny. Mr. Moreno is a ² _____. He takes pet pictures. He sees many dogs and cats every day. I went to his studio. He showed me cool cameras. Ms. Adame works at a restaurant. She brings food to ³ _____. She loves to talk to them. She said it is fun to hear different stories. Ms. Mayo is a teacher. She teaches first and third grade math. Her students are very smart. They read a lot. Lastly, Mr. Kinny is a ⁴ _____. He ⁵ _____ the town every day. He wears a cool ⁶ _____ to work. I spoke to these four people. Then I wrote a short essay about my future job. I want to meet many people, like Ms. Adame does. I also want to help others, like Mr. Kinny does. Oh, I don't know what I want to do!

Word Bank

customers	unifom	costomers
uniform	protects	police officer
photographer	policeofficer	desided
decided	plotects	fotographer

 Listen. Pause. Say each sentence.

  MP3 B1-2G

Writing Practice

Write the words.

1 _____

n

His job is taking pictures.
He is a _____.

2 _____

n

ex A _____ buys things in stores.

3 _____

n

They keep the town safe.
They are _____s.

4 _____

v keep people safe

5 _____

n clothes for work,
school, or sports

These are _____s.

6 _____

v choose

Write the words in each blank.

Summary

I talked to _____ people. I talked to a _____, a

restaurant worker, a teacher, and a police officer. Then I wrote about my future

_____. What is my dream job? I do _____ know.

Word Puzzle

 Complete the word puzzle.

2↓
clothes for work, school, or sports
These are _____s.

1↓
A _____ buys things in stores.

5→
His job is taking pictures. He is a _____.

4↓
choose

3↓
They keep the town safe.
They are _____s.

5↓
keep people safe

UNIT 3

Volunteering for the Community

Teacher's Book p.52

Think! You are helping someone. Where are you?

UNIT 3 Volunteering for the Community

Are you bored sometimes? Do you want to help others to feel happy? Then volunteering is perfect for you! Volunteering means helping others in your free time. You will not get money when you volunteer, but you will feel great! There are many things you can do in your own neighborhood. First, you can clean the street. Some streets are very dirty because people throw trash on the ground. There are plastic cups, paper, gum, and many other things on the ground. You can pick up the trash and clean the street. Second, you can plant trees in your neighborhood. Your parents can help you buy and plant trees. Just ask them! You can volunteer to plant trees in your neighborhood. The trees will grow and the air will be cleaner. The neighborhood will look great, too. Finally, you can volunteer at a library. You can help neighbors find books. You can also help to put the books in their right place. Why not start today?

New Words

volunteer	free time
v help others for free	*n* not work time or school time

trash	plastic
n garbage	*adj*
	These things are plastic.

pick up	right
v	*adj* correct
He is picking up trash.	

Part A. Sentence Completion

1. Your friends can _____ you with your project.

   (A) help
   (B) helps
   (C) helped
   (D) helping

2. Don't forget to pick _____ the trash under the desk.

   (A) it
   (B) on
   (C) up
   (D) down

Part B. Situational Writing

3.

   The air is very _____.

   (A) soft
   (B) dirty
   (C) fresh
   (D) clean

4.

   Jina likes to volunteer by _____.

   (A) planting trees
   (B) helping babies
   (C) drawing pictures
   (D) cleaning the street

We are looking for volunteers for a seniors' Valentine's Day party.

Date & Time: 12 - 3 PM, February 14th

Place: Daisy Seniors' Home

Job: putting up balloons, wrapping gifts, decorating cakes, and cleaning up after the party

Please come and celebrate with us!

5. What is true about the party?

 (A) It is at 7 PM.

 (B) It is for children.

 (C) It is on February 13th.

 (D) It is held at a seniors' home.

6. What job will volunteers NOT do?

 (A) clean up

 (B) wrap gifts

 (C) put up posters

 (D) decorate cakes

Part D. General Reading and Retelling

Are you bored sometimes? Do you want to help others to feel happy? Then volunteering is perfect for you! Volunteering means helping others in your free time. You will not get money when you volunteer, but you will feel great! There are many things you can do in your own neighborhood. First, you can clean the street. Some streets are very dirty because people throw trash on the ground. There are plastic cups, paper, gum, and many other things on the ground. You can pick up the trash and clean the street. Second, you can plant trees in your neighborhood. Your parents can help you buy and plant trees. Just ask them! You can volunteer to plant trees in your neighborhood. The trees will grow and the air will be cleaner. The neighborhood will look great, too. Finally, you can volunteer at a _____. You can help neighbors find books. You can also help to put the books in their right place. Why not start today?

7. What is the best title for the passage?

   (A) Money Can Help Anyone

   (B) Be Helpful in Your Neighborhood

   (C) Stop Throwing Away Plastic Cups

   (D) Read More Books and Become Smart

8. According to the passage, what is true about volunteering?

   (A) It is very boring.

   (B) You can get money.

   (C) You can do it nearby.

   (D) It takes too much time.

9. How can planting trees help people?

   (A) The air will be cleaner.

   (B) They can sell more paper.

   (C) They become homes for birds.

   (D) The street will have less trash.

10. Fill in the blank with the most suitable word.

   (A) farm

   (B) library

   (C) candy shop

   (D) animal hospital

Listening Practice

 Listen and write.

  MP3 B1-3

Volunteering for the Community

Are you bored sometimes? Do you want to help others to feel happy? Then volunteering is perfect for you! Volunteering means helping others in your

__1._____ . You will not get money when you __2._____ , but you will feel great! There are many things you can do in your own neighborhood. First, you can clean the street. Some streets are very dirty because people throw __3._____ on the ground. There are __4._____ cups, paper, gum, and many other things on the ground. You can __5._____ the trash and clean the street. Second, you can plant trees in your neighborhood. Your parents can help you buy and plant trees. Just ask them! You can volunteer to plant trees in your neighborhood. The trees will grow and the air will be cleaner. The neighborhood will look great, too. Finally, you can volunteer at a library. You can help neighbors find books. You can also help to put the books in their __6._____ place. Why not start today?

Word Bank

plastik	pick up	flee time
pig up	volunteer	free time
bolunteer	plastic	trashes
trash	light	right

 Listen. Pause. Say each sentence.

  MP3 B1-3G

Writing Practice

 Write the words.

1 _____	2 _____
v help others for free	*n* not work time or school time

3 _____	4 _____
n garbage	*adj* These things are _____.

5 _____	6 _____
v He is _____ing _____ trash.	*adj* correct

 Write the words in each blank.

Summary

You can _____ in your neighborhood. You can pick up

_____. You can plant _____. You can also volunteer

at a _____.

Word Puzzle

 Complete the word puzzle.

3 ↓
These things are _____.

2 ↓
correct

1 ↓
not work time or school time

4 →
help others for free

5 →
garbage

6 →
He is _____ing _____ trash.

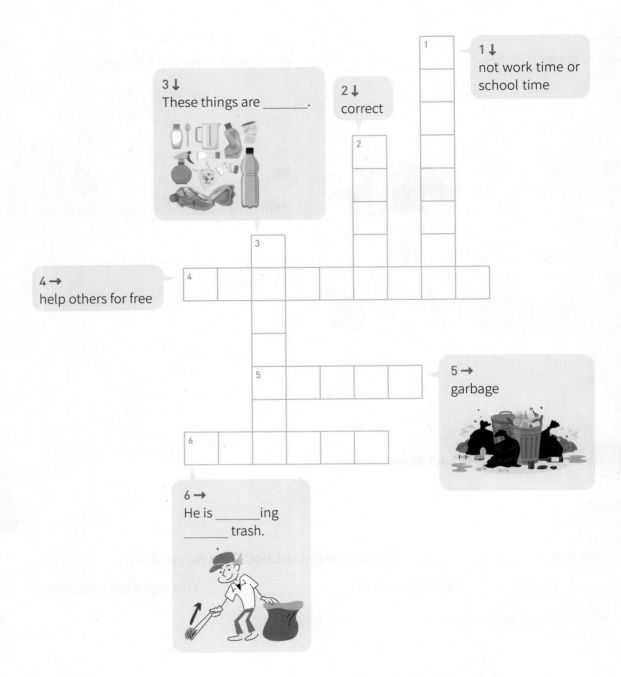

Teacher's Book
p.56

UNIT 4

A Great Man in Town

Think! Who needs your help? How can you help them?

Mr. Dawod is sixty years old, and he lives on Jewel Street. Everyone on Jewel Street knows him. Mr. Dawod is really popular. Why is he popular? First, he bakes bread in his kitchen on Mondays. Then, he takes the warm bread to his elderly neighbors. He visits his neighbors and talks to them. People enjoy his visits because he tells funny stories. Second, Mr. Dawod grows watermelons in summer. He takes the watermelons to families. The neighbors love Mr. Dawod's watermelons. The fruit is sweet and juicy. Third, every weekend, Mr. Dawod goes to the art gallery. He teaches drawing and coloring. Little kids use crayons, and adults use paint. They share the crayons and paint. Finally, Mr. Dawod feeds street cats every day. He makes different snacks for the cats, too. Mr. Dawod is the hero of our neighborhood!

New Words

popular *adj* **ex** Does everyone like him? Then he is <u>popular</u>.	**warm** *adj* just a little hot
elderly *adj* old	**juicy** *adj* full of juice
share *v* give some to everyone	**hero** *n* **ex** Some people really needed help. You helped them. You are a <u>hero</u>!

Part A. Sentence Completion

1. Everyone _____ this song.

    (A) know

    (B) knows

    (C) known

    (D) knowing

2. That juice _____ delicious!

    (A) is

    (B) am

    (C) did

    (D) were

Part B. Situational Writing

3.

    In summer, kids _____.

    (A) swim in the lake

    (B) play in the snow

    (C) sing at the beach

    (D) hike up the mountain

4.

    Mr. Barton and his dog are _____.

    (A) young

    (B) sitting

    (C) elderly

    (D) jumping

7 Ways to Make Others Happy

1. Listen to their stories.
2. Send letters or text messages to say hi.
3. Help them carry something heavy.
4. Exercise together.
5. Smile.
6. Share what you know with others.
7. Remember their birthday.

5. Which of these is on the list?

(A) Host parties.

(B) Help write letters.

(C) Give others money.

(D) Play sports together.

6. Ava and Kai are best friends. Kai got a bad grade in his math test today. He looked sad. Ava told him how to be good at math. Then, Kai was no longer sad. From the list items above, which can explain what Ava did?

(A) 1

(B) 3

(C) 5

(D) 6

Listening Practice

  MP3 B1-4

A Great Man in Town

Mr. Dawod is sixty years old, and he lives on Jewel Street. Everyone on Jewel Street knows him. Mr. Dawod is really ¹_____. Why is he popular? First, he bakes bread in his kitchen on Mondays. Then, he takes the ²_____ bread to his ³_____ neighbors. He visits his neighbors and talks to them. People enjoy his visits because he tells funny stories. Second, Mr. Dawod grows watermelons in summer. He takes the watermelons to families. The neighbors love Mr. Dawod's watermelons. The fruit is sweet and ⁴_____. Third, every weekend, Mr. Dawod goes to the art gallery. He teaches drawing and coloring. Little kids use crayons, and adults use paint. They ⁵_____ the crayons and paint. Finally, Mr. Dawod feeds street cats every day. He makes different snacks for the cats, too. Mr. Dawod is the ⁶_____ of our neighborhood!

Word Bank

popular	worm	pobular
hiro	juishy	sare
juicy	warm	elderry
hero	share	elderly

 Listen. Pause. Say each sentence.

  MP3 B1-4G

Writing Practice

A B C Write the words.

1 _____

adj

ex Does everyone like him? Then he is _____.

2 _____

adj just a little hot

3 _____

adj old

4 _____

adj full of juice

5 _____

v give some to everyone

6 _____

n

ex Some people really needed help. You helped them. You are a _____!

Write the words in each blank.

Summary

Mr. Dawod is popular in the neighborhood. He bakes _____ for elderly people. He gives families _____. He teaches people drawing and _____. And he feeds street _____.

Word Puzzle

 Complete the word puzzle.

1 →
give some to everyone

2 ↓
old

4 →
Some people really needed help. You helped them. You are a _____!

5 →
full of juice

6 →
just a little hot

3 ↓
Does everyone like him? Then he is _____.

CHAPTER REVIEW

The Axes

Teacher's Book p.60

A man had an axe[1] with a wooden[2] handle, but the axe fell in the river. The man cried. A fairy saw the problem. She went into the river. She returned with a golden[3] axe. "Is this your axe?" she asked the man. "No, it's not." said the man. The fairy went back into the river and returned with a silver axe. "Is this your axe?" she said. "No, it's not." said the man. The fairy went back into the river. She returned with the wooden axe. "Is this your axe?" she asked. "Yes, it is." the man said. "Keep all the axes." the fairy said. The man's neighbor heard the story. He wanted a golden axe, too. He threw his axe with a wooden handle into the river. The fairy entered the river and returned with a golden axe. "Is this your axe?" she asked the neighbor. The neighbor said, "Yes, it is." The fairy took the golden axe. "You get no axes now." she said. Then she left.

[1] axe    [2] wooden = made of wood
[3] golden = made of gold

CHAPTER 2

Neighborhood

UNIT 5

Kali's Favorite Park

 Teacher's Book p.61

Where is your favorite park? What can people do there?

Kali takes bus number 075 on the weekends. The bus takes her to her favorite place — Divo Park. The park is open from 6:00 AM to 11:00 PM. There are many people there, even in winter. Kali's favorite place in Divo Park is the Hamann Rose Garden. There are many roses in the garden. There is also a great fountain in the middle of the garden. Kali also loves the Sunken Garden. The Sunken Garden is the biggest garden in the city. There are roses, tulips, and many other types of flowers. Kali likes taking her dog to the park. The dog's name is Milo. Milo and Kali run around the park. It helps them stay healthy. When Kali feels thirsty, she goes to Juice Top. They sell delicious lemonade. She also gets water for Milo from Juice Top. Sometimes they feel sleepy in the park. They take a nap in the grass. They go home when the sun goes down. That's because it gets cold without sunlight.

New Words

favorite	**fountain**
adj	*n*
ex Is it your <u>favorite</u> thing? Then you like it the best.	**ex** A <u>fountain</u> has running water.
tulip	**healthy**
n	*adj* not sick
ex A <u>tulip</u> is a type of flower.	
delicious	**take a nap**
adj	*v* sleep a short time
ex Is it <u>delicious</u>? Then it tastes really good!	

Part A. Sentence Completion

 10 minutes

1. Bus number 10 _____ me to Union Square.

   (A) rides

   (B) takes

   (C) works

   (D) comes

2. John Peterson Hospital is the _____ hospital in town.

   (A) big

   (B) biggest

   (C) most big

   (D) more bigger

Part B. Situational Writing

3.

   Lee thinks the ice cream is _____.

   (A) hot

   (B) bad

   (C) bitter

   (D) delicious

4.

   I like to _____ during the day.

   (A) ride a bike

   (B) take a nap

   (C) walk my dog

   (D) clean my room

Dancing Dolphin Park

- **Children can play until 10 PM.**
- **No dogs allowed in the park.**

5. What are kids NOT doing in the park?

   (A) flying a kite

   (B) playing soccer

   (C) playing with sand

   (D) swimming in a pool

6. What is true about the park?

   (A) The park has two slides.

   (B) There are many dogs in the park.

   (C) It is called Sleeping Dolphin Park.

   (D) Children can play at 6 PM in the park.

Part D. General Reading and Retelling

Kali takes bus number 075 on the weekends. The bus takes her to her favorite place — Divo Park. The park is open from 6:00 AM to 11:00 PM. There are many people there, even in winter. Kali's favorite place in Divo Park is the Hamann Rose Garden. There are many roses in the garden. There is also a great fountain in the middle of the garden. Kali also loves the Sunken Garden. The Sunken Garden is the biggest garden in the city. There are roses, tulips, and many other types of flowers. Kali likes taking her dog to the park. The dog's name is Milo. Milo and Kali run around the park. It helps them stay healthy. When Kali feels thirsty, she goes to Juice Top. They sell delicious lemonade. She also gets water for Milo from Juice Top. Sometimes they feel sleepy in the park. They take a nap in the grass. They go home when the sun goes down. That's because it gets cold without sunlight.

7. What is the best title for the passage?

   (A) Fresh Juice Each Day
   (B) For Sale: Pretty Flowers
   (C) Divo Park: Kali's Favorite
   (D) Napping Contest at the Park

8. What does Kali do when the sun goes down?

   (A) go home
   (B) visit a garden
   (C) go to Juice Top
   (D) sleep in the grass

9. What is NOT true about Divo Park?

   (A) It is open to dogs.
   (B) It has many flowers.
   (C) It is closed during the winter.
   (D) It has a store called Juice Top.

10. What is Milo?

   (A) a bus
   (B) a dog
   (C) a garden
   (D) a fountain

Listening Practice

 Listen and write.

  MP3 B1-5

Kali's Favorite Park

Kali takes bus number 075 on the weekends. The bus takes her to her favorite place — Divo Park. The park is open from 6:00 AM to 11:00 PM. There are many people there, even in winter. Kali's ¹ _____ place in Divo Park is the Hamann Rose Garden. There are many roses in the garden. There is also a great ² _____ in the middle of the garden. Kali also loves the Sunken Garden. The Sunken Garden is the biggest garden in the city. There are roses, ³ _____ , and many other types of flowers. Kali likes taking her dog to the park. The dog's name is Milo. Milo and Kali run around the park. It helps them stay ⁴ _____ . When Kali feels thirsty, she goes to Juice Top. They sell ⁵ _____ lemonade. She also gets water for Milo from Juice Top. Sometimes they feel sleepy in the park. They ⁶ _____ in the grass. They go home when the sun goes down. That's because it gets cold without sunlight.

Word Bank

pountain	fountain	take a nap
delishus	tulips	favorite
delicious	healthy	tullips
takeanap	pavorite	helthy

 Listen. Pause. Say each sentence.

  MP3 B1-5G

Writing Practice

 Write the words.

1 _____

adj

ex Is it your _____ thing? Then you like it the best.

2 _____

n

ex A _____ has running water.

3 _____

n

ex A _____ is a type of flower.

4 _____

adj not sick

5 _____

adj

ex Is it _____? Then it tastes really good!

6 _____

v sleep a short time

 Write the words in each blank.

Summary

Kali likes Divo Park. She goes to a _____ garden. She and Milo the dog run around the _____. Sometimes Kali and Milo are _____. They drink juice and water. They take a _____ in the grass.

Word Puzzle

 Complete the word puzzle.

1 ↓
Is it your _____ thing?
Then you like it the best.

2 →
not sick

3 ↓
A _____ is a type of flower.

6 →
sleep a short time

4 ↓
A _____ has running water.

5 ↓
Is it _____?
Then it tastes really good!

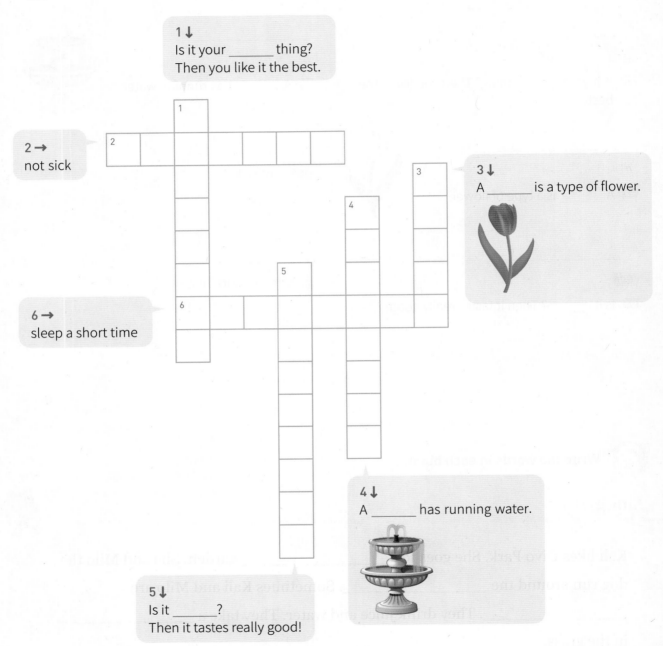

Teacher's Book
p.65

UNIT 6

Problems at the Mall

You are at the grocery store.
What do you put in your cart?

Alex enjoys grocery shopping with her parents. Last week, her family went to the supermarket in the mall. They needed food for Thanksgiving. They planned to cook a lot of food. Her mother wanted to buy some eggs, vegetables, beef, and fish. However, there was a problem at the supermarket. Her parents could not park their car. There were many cars in the parking lot. They waited in line for a long time. After they parked the car, they went into the mall. The mall also had too many people. Alex quickly put vegetables and beef into the cart. Her mother put fish into the cart. Then they paid for the food. Alex came home and looked at the food. Oh no! They did not buy eggs! She told her parents about the eggs. So her father walked to a small store. He bought ten eggs. He said, "Next time write a list. Then we will not forget the eggs."

New Words

grocery shopping
n buying fresh food at a supermarket or market

Thanksgiving
n an autumn holiday in Canada and the United States

vegetable
n

ex A carrot is a <u>vegetable</u>. Corn is a <u>vegetable</u>. Broccoli is a <u>vegetable</u>.

parking lot
n a place for many cars

wait in line
v stand in a line of people and wait

quickly
adv fast

Part A. Sentence Completion

1. Touma put a bottle of juice _____ his shopping cart.

   (A) at

   (B) off

   (C) into

   (D) through

2. Mom and Dad cook _____ food on Thanksgiving.

   (A) so

   (B) none

   (C) out of

   (D) a lot of

Part B. Situational Writing

3.
David ate his meat, but he will not eat his _____.

   (A) milk

   (B) fruit

   (C) sweets

   (D) vegetables

4.
_____ helps you remember things.

   (A) Writing a list

   (B) Asking friends

   (C) Calling parents

   (D) Teaching students

Song: "Shopping at the Store"
Artist: The Ice Cream Cones

We're shopping at the store.
We are shopping together.
I have a shopping cart.
What should I buy?

The vegetables look fresh!
They are purple, red, and white.
But look at that one! It is green! It is long!
I know what it is!
It's a _____!
Great! I love it!
Put one in the cart!

5. Which word is best for the blank?

(A) lemon

(B) tomato

(C) cucumber

(D) mushroom

6. What is NOT in the shopping cart?

(A) water

(B) bread

(C) a tomato

(D) a watermelon

Part D. General Reading and Retelling

Alex enjoys grocery shopping with her parents. Last week, her family went to the supermarket in the mall. They needed food for Thanksgiving. They planned to cook a lot of food. Her mother wanted to buy some eggs, vegetables, beef, and fish. However, there was a problem at the supermarket. Her parents could not park their car. There were many cars in the parking lot. They waited in line for a long time. After they parked the car, they went into the mall. The mall also had too many people. Alex quickly put vegetables and beef into the cart. Her mother put fish into the cart. Then they paid for the food. Alex came home and looked at the food. Oh no! _____ She told her parents about the eggs. So her father walked to a small store. He bought ten eggs. He said, "Next time write a list. Then we will not forget the eggs."

7. What is the passage mainly about?

(A) Alex's new car
(B) Alex's favorite hobby
(C) Alex's cooking mistake
(D) Alex's shopping problems

8. What was Alex's first problem?

(A) She could not find eggs.
(B) She got lost in the store.
(C) Her parents could not park.
(D) Her dad was alone in the car.

9. Which sentence is best for the blank?

(A) They did not buy eggs!
(B) There were a lot of people!
(C) They bought too much beef!
(D) There was no place to park!

10. How did Alex's dad get eggs?

(A) He went back to the farm.
(B) Alex's grandfather had some.
(C) There were eggs in the house.
(D) He found them in a small store.

Listening Practice

 Listen and write.

  MP3 B1-6

Problems at the Mall

Alex enjoys [1] shopping with her parents. Last week, her family went to the supermarket in the mall. They needed food for [2]. They planned to cook a lot of food. Her mother wanted to buy some eggs, [3], beef, and fish. However, there was a problem at the supermarket. Her parents could not park their car. There were many cars in the [4]. They [5] in line for a long time. After they parked the car, they went into the mall. The mall also had too many people. Alex [6] put vegetables and beef into the cart. Her mother put fish into the cart. Then they paid for the food. Alex came home and looked at the food. Oh no! They did not buy eggs! She told her parents about the eggs. So her father walked to a small store. He bought ten eggs. He said, "Next time write a list. Then we will not forget the eggs."

Word Bank

Tanksgiving	waited	quickly
vegtables	qickly	waded
paking lot	groshery	parking lot
grocery	vegetables	Thanksgiving

 Listen. Pause. Say each sentence.

  MP3 B1-6G

Writing Practice

 Write the words.

---

1 _____

  n   buying fresh food at a supermarket or market

2 _____

  n   an autumn holiday in Canada and the United States

---

3 _____

  n

  ex A carrot is a _____. Corn is a _____. Broccoli is a _____.

4 _____

  n   a place for many cars

---

5 _____

  v   stand in a line of people and wait

6 _____

  adv   fast

Write the words in each blank.

Summary

Alex's _____ went to the supermarket. They needed some eggs,

vegetables, beef, and _____. There were many cars in the

_____ lot. And they forgot the _____!

Word Puzzle

 Complete the word puzzle.

1 ↓
buying fresh food at a supermarket or market

2 →
fast

3 ↓
A carrot is a _____.
Corn is a _____.
Broccoli is a _____.

5 ↓
an autumn holiday in Canada and the United States

6 →
stand in a line of people and wait

4 ↓
a place for many cars

UNIT 7

Teacher's Book
p.69

A Horror Movie

What kind of movies do you like?
Can you watch horror movies?

UNIT (7) A Horror Movie

Takaya and I are best friends. We both like horror movies. We go to the movies every week in summer. We love many kinds of movies, but one movie is the scariest. It is a horror movie called "Martinez in Japan". It is about a boy named Grant Martinez. He studies in Japan. One day he was on the subway with his best friend, Yuri. He was going home from school. Suddenly, the subway stopped. People were very scared. Grant and Yuri were scared, too. The lights went out. People ran to the doors, but the doors stayed closed. No one could open them. Then someone said, "Look! There is a woman!" Everyone looked. There was a woman in a white dress. She was not in the subway car. She was standing on the station platform. People screamed, "Help!" Grant tried to break the door, but nothing happened! Do you want to know how the movie ended? Then you should watch the movie!

New Words

horror movie *n* **ex** Does the movie have monsters in it? Maybe it is a <u>horror movie</u>.	**scary** *adj* The horror movie is <u>scary</u>. So Mr. Pear is hiding behind his chair.
scared *adj* Mr. Pear is watching a horror movie. He is <u>scared</u>. So he is hiding behind his chair.	**the lights go out** **ex** The lights were on. But then the room was dark. <u>The lights went out</u>.
station platform *n* They are not in the subway car. They are on the <u>platform</u>. 	**scream** *v* **ex** Were you scared? Did you make a loud sound? Then you <u>scream</u>ed! 

Part A. Sentence Completion

1. Jamal read a book _____ "Happy Life".

   (A) call
   (B) calls
   (C) called
   (D) calling

2. Lily told _____ how the TV show ended.

   (A) he
   (B) me
   (C) she
   (D) they

Part B. Situational Writing

3.    The boy was _____ in the dark room.

   (A) glad
   (B) lucky
   (C) happy
   (D) scared

4.    My uncle is the man _____ the blue suit.

   (A) in
   (B) on
   (C) at
   (D) to

5. What is true according to the advertisement?

    (A) You must bring snacks.

    (B) The movie starts at 7 PM.

    (C) Children under 6 can get in.

    (D) The movie title is 'Master Cats.'

6. How much are tickets for 2 adults and 1 student?

    (A) $12

    (B) $14

    (C) $20

    (D) $22

Part D. General Reading and Retelling

Takaya and I are best friends. We both like horror movies. We go to the movies every week in summer. We love many kinds of movies, but one movie is the scariest. It is a horror movie called "Martinez in Japan". It is about a boy named Grant Martinez. He studies in Japan. One day he was on the subway with his best friend, Yuri. He was going home from school. Suddenly, the subway stopped. People were very scared. Grant and Yuri were scared, too. The lights went out. People ran to the doors, but the doors stayed closed. No one could open them. Then someone said, "Look! There is a woman!" Everyone looked. There was a woman in a white dress. She was not in the subway car. She was standing on the station platform. People screamed, "Help!" Grant tried to break the door, but nothing happened! Do you want to know how the movie ended? Then you should watch the movie!

7. What is the best title for the passage?

   (A) Grant Is Scared

   (B) A Very Scary Movie

   (C) Takaya Lives in Japan

   (D) A Schoolboy Saves the Day

8. Who is the writer's best friend?

   (A) Yuri

   (B) Grant

   (C) Takaya

   (D) Martinez

9. What is NOT true about Grant?

   (A) He is Yuri's brother.

   (B) He is studying in Japan.

   (C) He tried to break the door.

   (D) He took the subway with Yuri.

10. Why is Grant on the subway?

   (A) He is going home.

   (B) He is going to work.

   (C) He is going to school.

   (D) He is going to a hospital.

🎧 Listen and write.

MP3 B1-7

A Horror Movie

Takaya and I are best friends. We both like __1__ movies. We go to the movies every week in summer. We love many kinds of movies, but one movie is the __2__ . It is a horror movie called "Martinez in Japan". It is about a boy named Grant Martinez. He studies in Japan. One day he was on the subway with his best friend, Yuri. He was going home from school. Suddenly, the subway stopped. People were very __3__ . Grant and Yuri were scared, too. The __4__ went out. People ran to the doors, but the doors stayed closed. No one could open them. Then someone said, "Look! There is a woman!" Everyone looked. There was a woman in a white dress. She was not in the subway car. She was standing on the station __5__ . People __6__ , "Help!" Grant tried to break the door, but nothing happened! Do you want to know how the movie ended? Then you should watch the movie!

Word Bank

lights	scarriest	platform
holler	scared	rights
scariest	screamd	screamed
scarred	flatporm	horror

Listen. Pause. Say each sentence.

MP3 B1-7G

Writing Practice

 Write the words.

1 _____

n

ex Does the movie have monsters in it? Maybe it is a _____.

2 _____

adj

The horror movie is _____. So Mr. Pear is hiding behind his chair.

3 _____

adj

Mr. Pear is watching a horror movie. He is _____. So he is hiding behind his chair.

4 _____

ex The lights were on. But then the room was dark. _____.

5 _____

n

They are not in the subway car. They are on the _____.

6 _____

v

ex Were you scared? Did you make a loud sound? Then you _____ed!

 Write the words in each blank.

Summary

Takaya and I like _____ movies. "Martinez in Japan" is the _____ movie. In the movie, people are on a _____. The subway stops. But one _____ is still on the platform.

Word Puzzle

 Complete the word puzzle.

3 ↓

Mr. Pear is watching a horror movie. He is _____. So he is hiding behind his chair.

2 ↓

Were you scared? Did you make a loud sound? Then you _____ed!

5 →

Does the movie have monsters in it? Maybe it is a _____.

4 ↓

The lights were on. But then the room was dark. _____.

6 →

The horror movie is _____. So Mr. Pear is hiding behind his chair.

1 ↓

They are not in the subway car. They are on the _____.

UNIT 8

Teacher's Book
p.77

The Best Library in the City

Is there a library in your neighborhood?
What can you do there?

Elmwood Library is the best library in my city. It is big. It has three floors. It is open from 7:00 AM to 11:00 PM. More than 2000 people can read and study there. Only members can use the library. Everyone in my family is a member. My family goes to Elmwood Library every week. There are many books on the first floor. You can borrow up to 10 books at a time. You must bring them back in two weeks. There are 100 desks on the third floor. Students study there every day. On the second floor, library members can try different programs. Last month, the programs were "Summer Lunch," "Singalong Cinema," "Storytime with Dad," and "Book Quiz." Forty people can go to each event. I went to "Singalong Cinema" with my dad and sister. There were 25 kids and 15 adults. We sang "Candy Store," a song from a musical. We practiced four times. Next Saturday, we will sing in front of the whole city! I am very happy. But my sister is shy, so she is very worried. I want to cheer her up.

New Words

floor	**member**
n	*n*
ex Does the building have 30 <u>floors</u>? Then it is tall!	**ex** Did you join a club? Then you are a club <u>member</u>.
borrow X	**at a time**
v take X for free and then return X	*adv* each time
shy	**cheer somebody up**
adj quiet and scared in front of people	*v* make someone scared or sad feel better

Part A. Sentence Completion

1. At the park, _____ is happy.

   (A) two cats

   (B) everyone

   (C) my parents

   (D) Lily and James

2. You can use my crayons. Just bring _____ back tomorrow.

   (A) it

   (B) they

   (C) their

   (D) them

Part B. Situational Writing

3.

   The dog is _____ its house.

   (A) in

   (B) above

   (C) behind

   (D) in front of

4.

   I'm sorry Ella is sad. Let's _____.

   (A) start a fight

   (B) wake her up

   (C) cheer her up

   (D) find her shoes

Schedule for the first week of June

	Summer Lunch	Singalong Cinema	Storytime with Dad	Book Quiz
Date	June 3rd & 5th	June 2nd	June 6th	June 2nd & 4th
Time	1 PM	3 PM	3 PM	4 PM
Place	Front Yard	Benford Hall	Benford Hall	McGuire Auditorium
The number of open spots	6	2	8	12

5. Which program starts at 3 PM on June 6th?

(A) *Summer Lunch*

(B) *Singalong Cinema*

(C) *Storytime with Dad*

(D) *Book Quiz*

6. Which program can a group of 10 people go to?

(A) *Summer Lunch*

(B) *Singalong Cinema*

(C) *Storytime with Dad*

(D) *Book Quiz*

Part D. General Reading and Retelling

Elmwood Library is the best library in my city. It is big. It has three floors. It is open from 7:00 AM to 11:00 PM. More than 2000 people can read and study there. Only members can use the library. Everyone in my family is a member. My family goes to Elmwood Library every week. There are many books on the first floor. You can borrow up to 10 books at a time. You must bring them back in two weeks. There are 100 desks on the third floor. Students study there every day. On the second floor, library members can try different programs. Last month, the programs were "Summer Lunch," "Singalong Cinema," "Storytime with Dad," and "Book Quiz." Forty people can go to each event. I went to "Singalong Cinema" with my dad and sister. There were 25 kids and 15 adults. We sang "Candy Store," a song from a musical. We practiced four times. Next Saturday, we will sing in front of the whole city! I am very happy. But my sister is shy, so she is very worried. I want to cheer her up.

7. What is the main idea of the passage?

   (A) Elmwood Library is great.

   (B) Only members can use the library.

   (C) People don't like library programs.

   (D) Adults can sing in front of the whole city.

8. How many desks are on the third floor?

   (A) 25

   (B) 40

   (C) 100

   (D) 2000

9. According to the passage, what is NOT true about the library?

   (A) People can sing there.

   (B) Desks are on the third floor.

   (C) There are many programs at the library.

   (D) Members can borrow 12 books at a time.

10. Why is the writer's sister worried?

   (A) She has to study on the third floor.

   (B) She will go to programs at the library.

   (C) She will sing in front of the whole city.

   (D) She has to borrow 15 books at the same time.

Listen and write.

MP3 B1-8

The Best Library in the City

Elmwood Library is the best library in my city. It is big. It has three

¹ [_____]. It is open from 7:00 AM to 11:00 PM. More than 2000

people can read and study there. Only ² [_____] can use the library.

Everyone in my family is a member. My family goes to Elmwood Library every

week. There are many books on the first floor. You can ³ [_____] up

to 10 books ⁴ [_____]. You must bring them back in two weeks. There

are 100 desks on the third floor. Students study there every day. On the second

floor, library members can try different programs. Last month, the programs

were "Summer Lunch," "Singalong Cinema," "Storytime with Dad," and "Book

Quiz." Forty people can go to each event. I went to "Singalong Cinema" with my

dad and sister. There were 25 kids and 15 adults. We sang "Candy Store," a song

from a musical. We practiced four times. Next Saturday, we will sing in front

of the whole city! I am very happy. But my sister is ⁵ [_____], so she is

very worried. I want to ⁶ [_____] her up.

Word Bank

boro	at a time	mimbers
cheer	floor	borrow
shy	floors	chir
members	atatime	chy

Listen. Pause. Say each sentence.

MP3 B1-8G

Writing Practice

 Write the words.

1 _____

n

ex Does the building have 30 _____s? Then it is tall!

2 _____

n

ex Did you join a club? Then you are a club _____.

3 _____ X

v take X for free and then return X

4 _____

adv each time

5 _____

adj quiet and scared in front of people

6 _____ somebody _____

v make someone scared or sad feel better

Write the words in each blank.

Summary

Elmwood _____ is the best library in my city. My family goes there _____. There are books and study _____. There are special _____. I am in one program. I will sing.

Word Puzzle

 Complete the word puzzle.

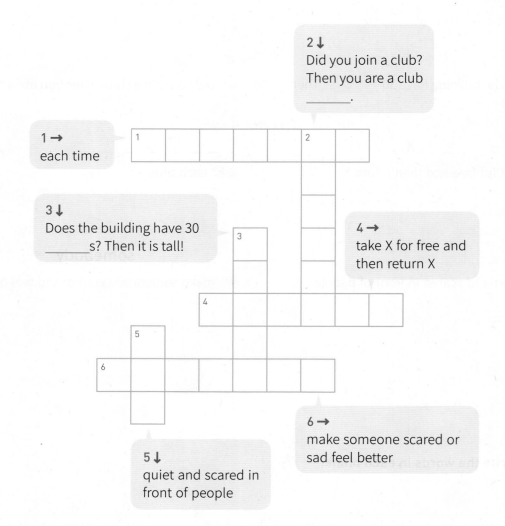

2 ↓
Did you join a club?
Then you are a club
_____.

1 →
each time

3 ↓
Does the building have 30
_____s? Then it is tall!

4 →
take X for free and
then return X

6 →
make someone scared or
sad feel better

5 ↓
quiet and scared in
front of people

At My Uncle's Bakery

Teacher's Book p.77

Every day before school, I stop by my uncle's bakery. He wakes up very early, so he can open it before 7 o'clock. Many students and business people come in to eat breakfast. The people stand in line and choose from the many types of bread. From seven to ten, customers can also buy coffee. After they pay at the counter, they eat very quickly. Sometimes I help make the sandwiches. I wrap them and take them to the front of the store. The most popular sandwich has bacon, lettuce, and tomato. The least popular is tuna, but I like it. My uncle's store always smells like delicious bread, because he bakes all day long. When I have to leave, my uncle always gives me a fresh chocolate chip cookie. I eat the warm and soft cookie as I walk to school.

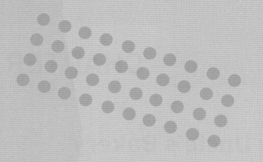

CHAPTER 3

Stadium in My Town

Teacher's Book
p.78

UNIT 9

At the Baseball Game

Do you like watching baseball?
Do you have a favorite team?

Maria's grandfather loves baseball. He likes a team called the Norton Lions. Yesterday Maria and her grandfather went to a baseball stadium. The Norton Lions and Upland Foxes were playing against each other. Maria and her grandfather wore orange t-shirts to the game. That's because orange is the Norton Lions team color. In this game, Maria really wanted to catch a home run ball. Before the game started, Maria's grandfather bought her some chicken. They ate it during the game. Suddenly, a home run ball flew near their seats. Maria was excited, and she dropped her chicken. Maria tried to catch the ball, but she was too slow. A big man caught the ball, and Maria was sad. Her grandfather said, "Let's try to catch another ball!" Sadly, there were no more home runs. The game ended after four hours. Then, her grandfather told her to open his bag. She opened it, and there was a ball. He told her, "Take it to the player over there!" The player signed the ball. Maria felt great.

New Words

baseball stadium *n* a big building to play baseball 	**home run** *n* going to all the bases in baseball 
drop *v*  He dropped the ball! Now the ball is on the ground.	**seat** *n* a place to sit
excited *adj* very happy	**sign X** *v* put your name on X

Part A. Sentence Completion

1. I tried to get tickets, _____ there were no more tickets.

   (A) so
   (B) for
   (C) but
   (D) and

2. Let's try to _____ that tree!

   (A) climb
   (B) climbs
   (C) climbed
   (D) climbing

Part B. Situational Writing

3.

Tina _____ her food.

   (A) ate
   (B) served
   (C) cooked
   (D) dropped

4.

Thomas is _____.

   (A) throwing a ball
   (B) catching a ball
   (C) watching baseball
   (D) buying baseball tickets

Profile

Abraham Mendez

Age: 23
Team: Norton Lions
Position: Pitcher
Uniform Number: 19
Hometown: Mexico City, Mexico

Profile

Hyun Oh

Age: 20
Team: Upland Foxes
Position: Left Fielder
Uniform Number: 8
Hometown: Los Angeles, USA

5. What is true about Hyun Oh?

   (A) He is a pitcher.

   (B) He is 23 years old.

   (C) He is from Los Angeles.

   (D) His uniform number is 19.

6. Which player plays for the Lions?

   (A) both

   (B) none

   (C) Hyun Oh

   (D) Abraham Mendez

Part D. General Reading and Retelling

Maria's grandfather loves baseball. He likes a team called the Norton Lions. Yesterday Maria and her grandfather went to a baseball stadium. The Norton Lions and Upland Foxes were playing against each other. Maria and her grandfather wore orange t-shirts to the game. That's because orange is the Norton Lions team color. In this game, Maria really wanted to catch a home run ball. Before the game started, Maria's grandfather bought her some chicken. They ate it during the game. Suddenly, a home run ball flew near their seats. Maria was excited, and she dropped her chicken. Maria tried to catch the ball, but she was too slow. A big man caught the ball, and Maria was sad. Her grandfather said, "Let's try to catch another ball!" Sadly, there were no more home runs. The game ended after four hours. Then, her grandfather told her to open his bag. She opened it, and there was a ball. He told her, "Take it to the player over there!" The player signed the ball. Maria felt great.

7. What is the best title of the passage?

   (A) A Nice Baseball Player
   (B) Maria's Day at the Stadium
   (C) A Big Man Steals Maria's Ball
   (D) Grandfather Loves the Upland Foxes

8. How long was the game?

   (A) 1 hour
   (B) 2 hours
   (C) 3 hours
   (D) 4 hours

9. Why did Maria wear an orange t-shirt?

   (A) It is the only t-shirt she had.
   (B) It is the color of the Norton Lions.
   (C) It is the color of the Upland Foxes.
   (D) It is her grandfather's favorite color.

10. What did Maria do when the ball flew near her?

   (A) ate more chicken
   (B) dropped her chicken
   (C) caught the home run ball
   (D) opened her grandfather's bag

Listening Practice

 Listen and write.

  MP3 B1-9

At the Baseball Game

Maria's grandfather loves baseball. He likes a team called the Norton Lions.

Yesterday Maria and her grandfather went to a baseball ¹_____ .
The Norton Lions and Upland Foxes were playing against each other. Maria
and her grandfather wore orange t-shirts to the game. That's because orange
is the Norton Lions team color. In this game, Maria really wanted to catch a
²_____ ball. Before the game started, Maria's grandfather bought
her some chicken. They ate it during the game. Suddenly, a home run ball
flew near their ³_____ . Maria was ⁴_____ , and she
⁵_____ her chicken. Maria tried to catch the ball, but she was too
slow. A big man caught the ball, and Maria was sad. Her grandfather said, "Let's
try to catch another ball!" Sadly, there were no more home runs. The game
ended after four hours. Then, her grandfather told her to open his bag. She
opened it, and there was a ball. He told her, "Take it to the player over there!"
The player ⁶_____ the ball. Maria felt great.

Word Bank

home runn	droped	staddium
signed	stadium	sined
home run	sits	excited
seats	dropped	exited

 Listen. Pause. Say each sentence.

  MP3 B1-9G

Writing Practice

 Write the words.

1 _____

 n a big building to play baseball

2 _____

n going to all the bases in baseball

3 _____

v He _____ped the ball! Now the ball is on the ground.

4 _____

n a place to sit

5 _____

adj very happy

6 _____ X

v put your name on X

📄 **Write the words in each blank.**

Summary

Maria and her grandfather went to a baseball _____. They wore _____ t-shirts. They ate _____. Maria did not catch a home run ball. But a player _____ her ball.

Word Puzzle

 Complete the word puzzle.

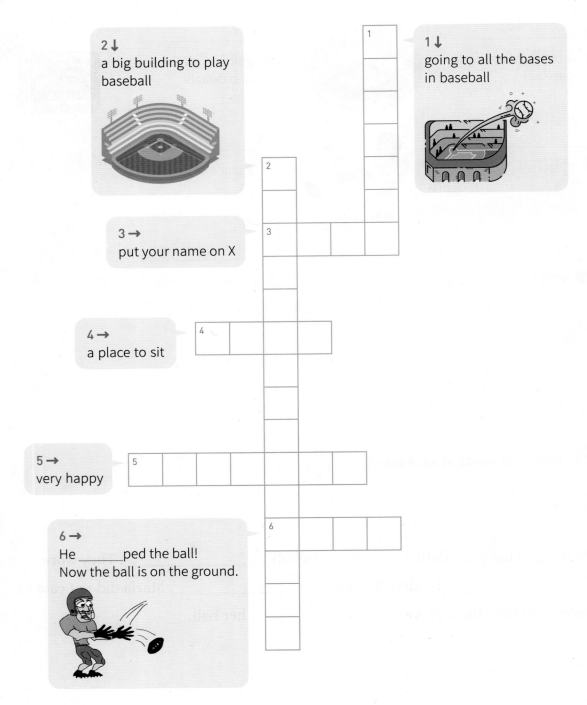

2 ↓
a big building to play baseball

1 ↓
going to all the bases in baseball

3 →
put your name on X

4 →
a place to sit

5 →
very happy

6 →
He _____ped the ball!
Now the ball is on the ground.

Teacher's Book
p.82

UNIT 10

A Favorite Sports Star

Do you know any famous sports stars?
Which sports do they play?

Minho wants to be a writer in the future. He wants to write books about sports stars. His favorite sports star is Alba Montalo. Alba Montalo was born in 1988. She started skating when she was seven. After three years, she was the best skater in her town. At 17, she was a Junior national champion in figure skating. When she was 19, she won the gold medal at the Senior National Games. Four years after that, she won the gold medal at the International Games. Minho loves Alba Montalo for two reasons. First, she is a great skater. She jumps and dances very well. Minho also likes Alba because she has a kind heart. She gives money to sick people. She helps younger skaters by teaching them new moves. She also plants trees in the summer. She even helps dogs on the streets. She tries to make everyone happy. Minho says Alba Montalo is inspiring. So he is working hard to become a writer. He plans to write books about people like Alba Montalo.

New Words

national	champion
adj at the country level	*n* winner

reason	move
n why something is that way	*n* a dance movement

inspiring	hard
adj	*adv* with effort
ex Does it make you want to be better? Then it is <u>inspiring</u>!	**ex** Do you study every day? Then you are working <u>hard</u>!

Part A. Sentence Completion

1. Jinsu _____ in 1997.

   (A) born

   (B) is born

   (C) was born

   (D) were born

2. Fatima trained her dogs. She taught _____ to dance.

   (A) it

   (B) his

   (C) our

   (D) them

Part B. Situational Writing

3.

Hyun is working hard to _____.

   (A) ride a bike

   (B) sing a song

   (C) write a book

   (D) play the trumpet

4.

Marta became a national _____.

   (A) loser

   (B) writer

   (C) skater

   (D) champion

| Profile | Biography | Achievements | Awards | Gallery | Videos |

Season 2007 - 2008

DATE	EVENTS	TOTAL SCORE
January 10	2007 World Championships	180.90
February 13	2007 Winter Olympic Games	214.23
December 3	2007 Grand Prix Final	192.34
October 19	2008 Grand Prix Skate Africa	215.08
November 13	2008 Grand Prix Skate South Africa	194.17

5. What was the total score of Alba Montalo in the 2007 Winter Olympic Games?

(A) 180.90

(B) 214.23

(C) 192.34

(D) 215.08

6. In which event did Alba Montalo score the lowest?

(A) 2007 Grand Prix Final

(B) 2007 World Championships

(C) 2008 Grand Prix Skate Africa

(D) 2008 Grand Prix Skate South Africa

Part D. General Reading and Retelling

Minho wants to be a writer in the future. He wants to write books about sports stars. His favorite sports star is Alba Montalo. Alba Montalo was born in 1988. She started skating when she was seven. After three years, she was the best skater in her town. At 17, she was a Junior national champion in figure skating. When she was 19, she won the gold medal at the Senior National Games. Four years after that, she won the gold medal at the International Games. Minho loves Alba Montalo for two reasons. First, she is a great skater. She jumps and dances very well. Minho also likes Alba because she has a _____ heart. She gives money to sick people. She helps younger skaters by teaching them new moves. She also plants trees in the summer. She even helps dogs on the streets. She tries to make everyone happy. Minho says Alba Montalo is inspiring. So he is working hard to become a writer. He plans to write books about people like Alba Montalo.

7. How old was Alba Montalo when she won at the Senior National Games?

(A) 17

(B) 19

(C) 21

(D) 23

8. What is Minho's dream?

(A) to become a writer

(B) to become a dancer

(C) to become a figure skater

(D) to become a medal winner

9. What is the best word for the blank?

(A) cold

(B) kind

(C) mean

(D) smart

10. What is probably true about Alba Montalo?

(A) She dislikes jumping.

(B) She prefers cats to dogs.

(C) She enjoys helping people.

(D) She won a skating medal in 1988.

Listening Practice

 Listen and write.

  MP3 B1-10

A Favorite Sports Star

Minho wants to be a writer in the future. He wants to write books about sports stars. His favorite sports star is Alba Montalo. Alba Montalo was born in 1988. She started skating when she was seven. After three years, she was the best skater in her town. At 17, she was a Junior ¹_____ ²_____ in figure skating. When she was 19, she won the gold medal at the Senior National Games. Four years after that, she won the gold medal at the International Games. Minho loves Alba Montalo for two ³_____. First, she is a great skater. She jumps and dances very well. Minho also likes Alba because she has a kind heart. She gives money to sick people. She helps younger skaters by teaching them new ⁴_____. She also plants trees in the summer. She even helps dogs on the streets. She tries to make everyone happy. Minho says Alba Montalo is ⁵_____. So he is working ⁶_____ to become a writer. He plans to write books about people like Alba Montalo.

Word Bank

champion	enspiring	national
reasons	mobes	moves
chammpion	inspiring	leasons
nashional	hard	had

 Listen. Pause. Say each sentence.

  MP3 B1-10G

Writing Practice

ABC Write the words.

---

1 _____

　adj　at the country level

2 _____

　n　winner

---

3 _____

　n　why something is that way

4 _____

　n　a dance movement

---

5 _____

　adj

　ex Does it make you want to be better? Then it is _____!

6 _____

　adv　with effort

　ex Do you study every day? Then you are working _____!

📄 Write the words in each blank.

Summary

Minho's favorite _____ star is Alba Montalo. There are two

_____. First, she is a great _____. Second, she is

_____.

Word Puzzle

 Complete the word puzzle.

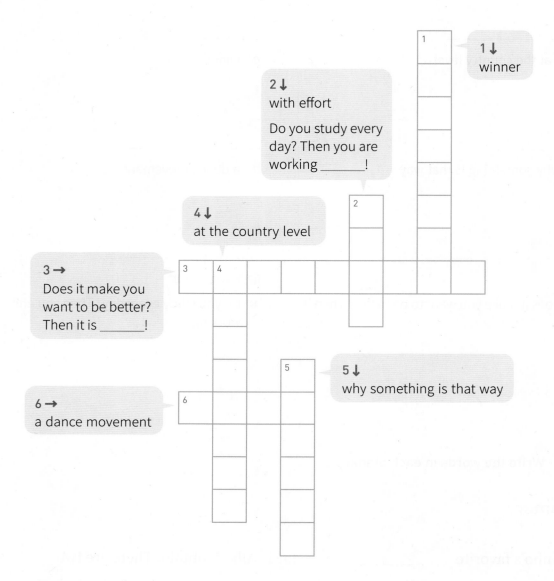

1↓ winner

2↓ with effort

Do you study every day? Then you are working _____!

4↓ at the country level

3→ Does it make you want to be better? Then it is _____!

5↓ why something is that way

6→ a dance movement

UNIT 11

 Teacher's Book p.86

A Magic Show

Do you like magic shows? Can you do a magic trick?

Yuran Lee is a famous magician. He uses cards, rabbits, and birds in his show. Every year he has a magic show at a stadium. In my town there is a big arena. It is called Palmer Arena. More than 20,000 people can go into the stadium. That's much bigger than my school! My sister loves Yuran Lee. She goes to Palmer Arena to see Yuran Lee every year. This year, the concert is on June 8th. My sister is very excited. Her friends Adam and Caleb are also going. Adam and Caleb love watching magic shows, too. My dad will drive them all to the stadium. He and my sister will first pick up Adam on Q Street. Then, they will go to Caleb's house on Almis Street. The stadium is on Bole Street. After the show, they will go to Panes. Panes is a restaurant. They sell chicken strips. I love chicken strips, so my dad is taking me, too. I am so excited about the show!

New Words

magician n  Is magic his job? Then he is a <u>magician</u>.	**arena** n a big building for sports and concerts
be called v ex <u>Is</u> it <u>called</u> Palmer Arena? Then Palmer Arena is its name!	**magic show** n a concert by a magician
pick up X v ex Did the father <u>pick up</u> his kids from the arena? Then he went to get them.	**chicken strips** n 

Part A. Sentence Completion

1. We have birthday cake every _____.

   (A) year

   (B) years

   (C) to year

   (D) for year

2. I love watermelon, _____ I have it every summer.

   (A) or

   (B) so

   (C) too

   (D) very

Part B. Situational Writing

3.    Two moms are _____ their children.

   (A) picking up

   (B) cycling toward

   (C) sitting down with

   (D) driving away from

4.    Lina and Bill are _____ to see the show.

   (A) bored

   (B) worried

   (C) excited

   (D) unhappy

Concert Ticket

Lee's 8th Magic Show

Date   **June 8th**

Time   **2 PM**

Place   **Palmer Arena**

Ticket Price   **At the ticket office (May 20th - June 7th): $15**

                    At the door: $20

5. What is NOT true about the show?

(A) It is at 2 PM.

(B) It is on June 5th.

(C) It is a magic show.

(D) It is held at Palmer Arena.

6. How can you get a ticket for 15 dollars?

(A) Buy it online.

(B) Buy it with Lee.

(C) Buy it at the door.

(D) Buy it before June 8th.

Part D. General Reading and Retelling

Yuran Lee is a famous magician. He uses cards, rabbits, and birds in his show. Every year he has a magic show at a stadium. In my town there is a big arena. It is called Palmer Arena. More than 20,000 people can go into the stadium. That's much bigger than my school! My sister loves Yuran Lee. She goes to Palmer Arena to see Yuran Lee every year. This year, the concert is on June 8th. My sister is very excited. Her friends Adam and Caleb are also going. Adam and Caleb love watching magic shows, too. My dad will drive them all to the stadium. He and my sister will first pick up Adam on Q Street. Then, they will go to Caleb's house on Almis Street. The stadium is on Bole Street. After the show, they will go to Panes. Panes is a restaurant. They sell chicken strips. I love chicken strips, so my dad is taking me, too. I am so excited about the show!

7. What is the passage mainly about?

   (A) a sister's magic performance

   (B) Yuran Lee's show at an arena

   (C) the delicious chicken at Panes

   (D) Palmer Arena's many concerts

8. What is NOT true about the Palmer Arena?

   (A) It is on Q Street.

   (B) It hosts magic shows.

   (C) It is bigger than the writer's school.

   (D) More than 20,000 people can use it.

9. How will the writer's sister go to the stadium?

   (A) by car

   (B) on foot

   (C) by bus

   (D) by bike

10. Who is Caleb?

   (A) Adam's brother

   (B) the writer's dad

   (C) the sister's friend

   (D) a worker at Panes

Listening Practice

 Listen and write.

  MP3 B1-11

A Magic Show

Yuran Lee is a famous ___1___ . He uses cards, rabbits, and birds in his show. Every year he has a ___2___ show at a stadium. In my town there is a big ___3___ . It is ___4___ Palmer Arena. More than 20,000 people can go into the stadium. That's much bigger than my school! My sister loves Yuran Lee. She goes to Palmer Arena to see Yuran Lee every year. This year, the concert is on June 8th. My sister is very excited. Her friends Adam and Caleb are also going. Adam and Caleb love watching magic shows, too. My dad will drive them all to the stadium. He and my sister will first ___5___ Adam on Q Street. Then, they will go to Caleb's house on Almis Street. The stadium is on Bole Street. After the show, they will go to Panes. Panes is a restaurant. They sell chicken strips. I love chicken ___6___ , so my dad is taking me, too. I am so excited about the show!

Word Bank

magic	magician	colled
stripes	majitian	arena
called	pick up	strips
pickup	arina	majic

 Listen. Pause. Say each sentence.

  MP3 B1-11G

Writing Practice

 Write the words.

1 _____

n

> Is magic his job?
> Then he is a _____.

2 _____

n a big building for sports and concerts

3 _____

v

ex _____ it _____ Palmer Arena? Then Palmer Arena is its name!

4 _____

n a concert by a magician

5 _____ X

v

ex Did the father _____ his kids from the arena? Then he went to get them.

6 _____

n

 Write the words in each blank.

Summary

Yuran Lee is a famous _____. My sister and her

_____ are going to his _____. After the show, they

will go to a _____ called Panes. I will go, too.

Word Puzzle

 Complete the word puzzle.

2 ↓

1 →
Is magic his job?
Then he is a _____.

3 →
a concert by a
magician

4 →
a big building for
sports and concerts

5 →
Did the father _____ his
kids from the arena? Then
he went to get them.

6 ↓
Is it _____ Palmer
Arena? Then Palmer
Arena is its name!

Teacher's Book
p.90

UNIT 12

Quiet Hip Hop Songs

What kind of music do you like? Why do you like it?

I had a fight with my best friend last week. Her name is Dori. She is a big fan of Billy Donley. Billy is a singer. He usually sings soft, slow songs. He plays guitar while he sings. I don't like slow songs. I also don't like the guitar. I love hip-hop because it's cool! I am a fan of Domar. He is a famous singer and rapper. Dori doesn't like Domar because she doesn't like hip-hop. That is why we fought. Dori said Domar's songs were dumb. I said Billy Donley's songs were bad. Dori and I did not talk for two days. Then, yesterday Dori told me about John Foy's new music. I listened to his songs. I was surprised. He sang hip-hop, but it was slow! Normally, I don't like slow songs, but I liked these ones. Dori told me she liked his songs, too. I bought John Foy's album. Now we are both fans of John Foy!

New Words

have a fight with

v argue with

be a big fan of X

v like X a lot

usually

adv most of the time

ex Ben usually goes to bed early. But today he is staying up late.

dumb

adj stupid

normally

adv most of the time

ex Mina normally brings her lunch. But today she is eating in a restaurant.

album

n a collection of music

Part A. **Sentence Completion**

1. Yuji _____ a great song at the concert yesterday.

   (A) sing

   (B) sang

   (C) sung

   (D) sings

2. My sister likes to _____ hip-hop music.

   (A) listen

   (B) listen to

   (C) listen at

   (D) listen by

Part B. **Situational Writing**

3.

   My best friend and I _____.

   (A) had a fight

   (B) used a fan

   (C) played the guitar

   (D) danced all morning

4.

   It's Joe's concert today. She has a lot of _____.

   (A) fans

   (B) bands

   (C) guitars

   (D) albums

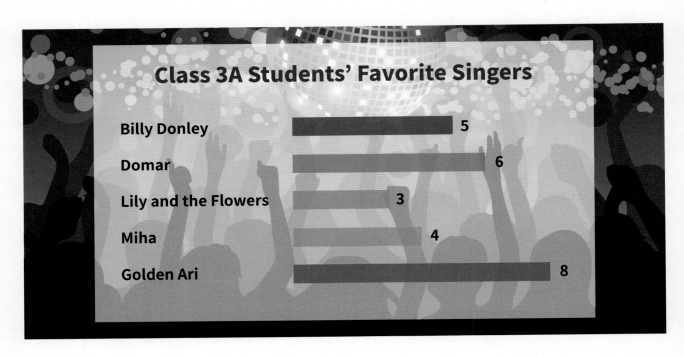

Class 3A Students' Favorite Singers

Billy Donley	5
Domar	6
Lily and the Flowers	3
Miha	4
Golden Ari	8

5. Which singer is the students' least favorite?

(A) Billy Donley

(B) Lily and the Flowers

(C) Miha

(D) Golden Ari

6. How many students like Miha?

(A) 3

(B) 4

(C) 6

(D) 8

Part D. General Reading and Retelling

I had a fight with my best friend last week. Her name is Dori. She is a big fan of Billy Donley. Billy is a singer. He usually sings soft, slow songs. He plays guitar while he sings. I don't like slow songs. I also don't like the guitar. I love hip-hop because it's cool! I am a fan of Domar. He is a famous singer and rapper. Dori doesn't like Domar because she doesn't like hip-hop. That is why we fought. Dori said Domar's songs were dumb. I said Billy Donley's songs were bad. Dori and I did not talk for two days. Then, yesterday Dori told me about John Foy's new music. I listened to his songs. I was surprised. He sang hip-hop, but it was slow! Normally, I don't like slow songs, but I liked these ones. Dori told me she liked his songs, too. I bought John Foy's album. Now we are both fans of John Foy!

7. Which is the best title for the passage?

(A) Music Is Great

(B) Good Friends Don't Fight

(C) I Want to Become Famous

(D) Finding Music We Both Like

8. Why did the writer fight with her friend?

(A) Her friend doesn't like sports.

(B) The writer lost her music player.

(C) They like different types of music.

(D) Her friend loves hip-hop very much.

9. Who does Dori like very much?

(A) Domar

(B) Dori Foy

(C) Billy Donley

(D) John Donley

10. What is NOT true about John Foy's songs?

(A) They are old.

(B) They are slow.

(C) Dori likes them.

(D) They are hip-hop music.

Listening Practice

 Listen and write.

  MP3 B1-12

Quiet Hip Hop Songs

I had a ¹ _____ with my best friend last week. Her name is Dori. She is a big ² _____ of Billy Donley. Billy is a singer. He ³ _____ sings soft, slow songs. He plays guitar while he sings. I don't like slow songs. I also don't like the guitar. I love hip-hop because it's cool! I am a fan of Domar. He is a famous singer and rapper. Dori doesn't like Domar because she doesn't like hip-hop. That is why we fought. Dori said Domar's songs were ⁴ _____. I said Billy Donley's songs were bad. Dori and I did not talk for two days. Then, yesterday Dori told me about John Foy's new music. I listened to his songs. I was surprised. He sang hip-hop, but it was slow! ⁵ _____, I don't like slow songs, but I liked these ones. Dori told me she liked his songs, too. I bought John Foy's ⁶ _____. Now we are both fans of John Foy!

Word Bank

fan	usually	fight
pite	Nomally	dumb
Normally	elbum	pan
usally	dum	album

 Listen. Pause. Say each sentence.

  MP3 B1-12G

Writing Practice

 Write the words.

1 _____

v argue with

2 _____ X

v like X a lot

⁴u_____

adv most of the time

ex Ben _____ goes to bed early. But today he is staying up late.

4 _____

adj stupid

⁵n_____

adv most of the time

ex Mina _____ brings her lunch. But today she is eating in a restaurant.

6 _____

n a collection of music

 Write the words in each blank.

Summary

My friend Dori and I had a _____. She likes slow songs. I like _____ hip-hop. Then Dori told me about John Foy. He sings _____ hip-hop. Both Dori and I are _____ of John Foy!

Word Puzzle

  Complete the word puzzle.

1 ↓

most of the time

Mina _____ brings her lunch. But today she is eating in a restaurant.

2 ↓

a collection of music

3 ↓

argue with

4 →

most of the time

Ben _____ goes to bed early. But today he is staying up late.

5 ↓

stupid

6 →

like X a lot

The Best Jumper

Teacher's Book p.94

One autumn day, Ms. Rabbit and Mr. Pig had a sports competition. They had one question: Who was the best jumper? They went near the stadium in their town. Behind the stadium there was some dirt. The dirt had a big hole. Ms. Rabbit said, "This is perfect. Let's see who is the best. Let's jump over the hole." Mr. Pig said, "I am sure I will be the winner. Just wait and see!" Ms. Rabbit and Mr. Pig lined up about one meter from the hole. Ms. Rabbit jumped first. She went quite far, but she fell into the hole. Then Mr. Pig jumped. He also fell into the hole but was a little bit behind Ms. Rabbit. Ms. Bear was watching the whole sports competition. Ms. Rabbit and Mr. Pig asked her, "Who do you think is the best?" Ms. Bear said to them, "Who is the best? I don't know. You are both in a hole."

ANSWERS

CHAPTER 1 | Neighbors
p.10

UNIT 1 ▶ B1-1 p.11

⏱ 1 (C) 2 (D) 3 (B) 4 (D) 5 (B) 6 (C) 7 (A) 8 (D) 9 (B) 10 (B)

🎧 1 neighbors 2 care 3 broke down 4 kind 5 worry 6 neighborhood

✏ 1 neighborhood 2 neighbor 3 care about 4 break down 5 kind 6 worry about

📄 neighbors, officers, is, live

▦ → 2 break down 4 care about 5 worry about 6 neighbor ↓ 1 kind 2 neighborhood

UNIT 2 ▶ B1-2 p.19

⏱ 1 (A) 2 (A) 3 (B) 4 (B) 5 (C) 6 (C) 7 (D) 8 (C) 9 (A) 10 (B)

🎧 1 decided 2 photographer 3 customers 4 police officer 5 protects 6 uniform

✏ 1 photographer 2 customer 3 police officer 4 protect 5 uniform 6 decide

📄 four, photographer, job, not

▦ → 5 photographer ↓ 1 customer 2 uniform 3 police officer 4 decide 5 protect

UNIT 3 ▶ B1-3 p.27

⏱ 1 (A) 2 (C) 3 (B) 4 (A) 5 (D) 6 (C) 7 (B) 8 (C) 9 (A) 10 (B)

🎧 1 free time 2 volunteer 3 trash 4 plastic 5 pick up 6 right

✏ 1 volunteer 2 free time 3 trash 4 plastic 5 pick up 6 right

📄 volunteer, trash, trees, library

▦ → 4 volunteer 5 trash 6 pick up ↓ 1 free time 2 right 3 plastic

UNIT 4 ▶ B1-4 p.35

⏱ 1 (B) 2 (A) 3 (A) 4 (C) 5 (D) 6 (D) 7 (D) 8 (C) 9 (D) 10 (D)

🎧 1 popular 2 warm 3 elderly 4 juicy 5 share 6 hero

✏ 1 popular 2 warm 3 elderly 4 juicy 5 share 6 hero

📄 bread, watermelon, coloring, cats

▦ → 1 share 4 hero 5 juicy 6 warm ↓ 2 elderly 3 popular

CHAPTER 2 | Neighborhood
p.44

UNIT 5 ▶ B1-5 p.45

⏱ 1 (B) 2 (B) 3 (D) 4 (B) 5 (D) 6 (D) 7 (C) 8 (A) **9 (C)** 10 (B)

🎧 1 favorite 2 fountain 3 tulips 4 healthy 5 delicious **6 take a nap**

✏ 1 favorite 2 fountain 3 tulip 4 healthy 5 delicious **6 take a nap**

📄 rose, park, thirsty, nap

▦ → 2 healthy 6 take a nap ↓ 1 favorite 3 tulip 4 fountain 5 delicious

UNIT 6 ▶ B1-6 p.53

⏱ 1 (C) 2 (D) 3 (D) 4 (A) 5 (C) 6 (D) 7 (D) 8 (C) 9 (A) 10 (D)

🎧 1 grocery 2 Thanksgiving 3 vegetables 4 parking lot 5 waited 6 quickly

✏ 1 grocery shopping 2 Thanksgiving 3 vegetable 4 parking lot 5 wait in line 6 quickly

📄 family, fish, parking, eggs

▦ → 2 quickly 6 wait in line ↓ 1 grocery shopping 3 vegetable 4 parking lot 5 Thanksgiving

UNIT 7 ▶ B1-7 p.61

⏱ 1 (C) 2 (B) 3 (D) 4 (A) 5 (B) 6 (D) 7 (B) 8 (C) 9 (A) 10 (A)

🎧 1 horror 2 scariest 3 scared 4 lights 5 platform 6 screamed

✏ 1 horror movie 2 scary 3 scared 4 the lights go out 5 station platform 6 scream

📄 horror, scariest, subway, woman

▦ → 5 horror movie 6 scary ↓ 1 station platform 2 scream 3 scared 4 the lights go out

UNIT 8 ▶ B1-8 p.69

⏱ 1 (B) 2 (D) 3 (D) 4 (C) 5 (C) 6 (D) 7 (A) 8 (C) 9 (D) 10 (C)

🎧 1 floors 2 members 3 borrow 4 at a time 5 shy 6 cheer

✏ 1 floor 2 member 3 borrow 4 at a time 5 shy 6 cheer, up

📄 Library, every week, desks, programs

▦ → 1 at a time 4 borrow 6 cheer up ↓ 2 member 3 floor 5 shy

CHAPTER 3 | Stadium in My Town
p.78

UNIT 9 ▶ B1-9 p.79

⏱ 1 (C) 2 (A) 3 (D) 4 (B) 5 (C) 6 (D) 7 (B) 8 (D) 9 (B) 10 (B)

🎧 1 stadium 2 home run 3 seats 4 excited 5 dropped 6 signed

✏ 1 baseball stadium 2 home run 3 drop 4 seat 5 excited 6 sign

📄 stadium, orange, chicken, signed

▦ → 3 sign 4 seat 5 excited 6 drop ↓ 1 home run 2 baseball stadium

UNIT 10 ▶ B1-10 p.87

⏱ 1 (C) 2 (D) 3 (C) 4 (D) 5 (B) 6 (B) 7 (B) 8 (A) 9 (B) 10 (C)

🎧 1 national 2 champion 3 reasons 4 moves 5 inspiring 6 hard

✏ 1 national 2 champion 3 reason 4 move 5 inspiring 6 hard

📄 sports, reasons, skater, kind

▦ → 3 inspiring 6 move ↓ 1 champion 2 hard 4 national 5 reason

UNIT 11 ▶ B1-11 p.95

⏱ 1 (A) 2 (B) 3 (A) 4 (C) 5 (B) 6 (D) 7 (B) 8 (A) 9 (A) 10 (C)

🎧 1 magician 2 magic 3 arena 4 called 5 pick up 6 strips

✏ 1 magician 2 arena 3 be called 4 magic show 5 pick up 6 chicken strips

📄 magician, friends, concert, restaurant

▦ → 1 magician 3 magic show 4 arena 5 pick up ↓ 2 chicken strips 6 called

UNIT 12 ▶ B1-12 p.103

⏱ 1 (B) 2 (B) 3 (A) 4 (A) 5 (B) 6 (B) 7 (D) 8 (C) 9 (C) 10 (A)

🎧 1 fight 2 fan 3 usually 4 dumb 5 Normally 6 album

✏ 1 have a fight with 2 be a big fan of 3 usually 4 dumb 5 normally 6 album

📄 fight, cool, slow, fans

▦ → 4 usually 6 be a big fan of ↓ 1 normally 2 album 3 have a fight with 5 dumb

엄선된 **100만 명**의 응시자 성적 데이터를 활용한 **AI기반** 데이터 공유 및 가치 고도화 **플랫폼**

TOSEL® Lab
국제토셀위원회 지정교육기관

공동기획
- 고려대학교 문과대학 언어정보연구소
- 국제토셀위원회

TOSEL Lab 국제토셀위원회 지정교육기관이란?

국내외 15,000여 개 학교·학원 단체응시인원 중 엄선한 100만 명 이상의 실제 TOSEL 성적 데이터와,
정부(과학기술정보통신부)의 AI 바우처 지원 사업 수행기관 선정으로 개발된 맞춤식 AI 빅데이터 기반 영어성장 플랫폼입니다.

진단평가를 통한 올바른 영어학습 방향 제시를 잘 할 수 있는 전국의 학원 및 단체를 찾아,
TOSEL Lab 지정교육기관으로 선정합니다. 선정된 기관들에게는 아래의 초도물품이 제공됩니다.

※ TOSEL Lab 지정교육기관에 제공되는 초도물품

Reading Series

내신과 **토셀 고득점**을 한꺼번에

Pre-Starter | Starter | Basic | Junior | High-Junior

- 각 단원 학습 도입부에 주제와 관련된 이미지를 통한 말하기 연습
- 각 Unit 별 4-6개의 목표 단어 제시, 그림 또는 영문으로 단어 뜻을 제공하여 독해 학습 전 단어 숙지
- 독해&실용문 연습을 위한 지문과 Comprehension 문항을 10개씩 수록하여 이해도 확인 및 진단
- 숙지한 독해 지문을 원어민 음성으로 들으며 듣기 학습 , 듣기 전, 듣기 중, 듣기 후 학습 커리큘럼 마련

Listening Series

한국 학생들에게 최적화된 듣기 실력 완성!

Pre-Starter | Starter | Basic | Junior | High-Junior

- 초등 / 중등 교과과정 연계 말하기&듣기 학습과 세분화된 레벨
- TOSEL 기출 문장과 실생활에 자주 활용되는 문장 패턴을 통해 듣기 및 말하기 학습
- 실제 TOSEL 지문의 예문을 활용한 실용적 학습 제공
- 실전 감각 향상과 점검을 위한 기출 문제 수록

Speaking Series

한국 학생들에게 최적화된 말하기 실력 완성!

Pre-Starter | Starter | Basic | Junior | High-Junior

- 단어 → 문법 → 표현 → 대화로 이어지는 단계적인 학습
- 교과과정에 연계한 설계로 내신과 수행평가 완벽 대비
- 최신 수능 출제 문항을 반영한 문장으로 수능 대비까지
- 전국 Speaking 올림피아드 공식 대비 교재